THE BALLOONISTS

THE BALLOONISTS BY EULA BISS

HANGING LOOSE PRESS
BROOKLYN, NEW YORK

Published by Hanging Loose Press, 231 Wyckoff Street, Brooklyn, NY 11217-2208. All rights reserved. No part of this book may be reproduced without the publisher's written permission, except for brief quotations in reviews.

www.hangingloosepress.com

Printed in the United States of America
10 9 8 7 6 5 4 3 2 1

Hanging Loose Press thanks the Literature Program of the New York State Council on the Arts for a grant in support of publication of this book.

Text and cover design by Benjamin Piekut.

Cover photograph – "The Breitling Orbiter 3 balloon touching down 70 kilometers north of the Egyptian desert town of Mut early Sunday, March 21, 1999. Swiss Betrand Piccard and Briton Brian Jones are the first avaitors to fly a hot air balloon around the world non-stop." –Agence France-Presse

Photograph of author by Anna Bernabe

Library of Congress Cataloging in Process information available on request.

ISBN 1-931236-07-0 (paperback)
ISBN 1-931236-08-9 (hardcover)

 Produced at The Print Center, Inc. 225 Varick St., New York, NY 10014, a non-profit facility for literary and arts-related publications. (212) 206-8465

For my sister, Mavis.
I wish you all-new mistakes.

Prelude: The Box

Mother: "I almost eloped once. When I was seventeen."

What happened?

Mother: "I got a very bad stomach ache and he left without me."

In the newspapers someone is always searching the ocean for a black box. A record of what was said by the pilots before the crash. The search for a black box can go on for weeks after the search for survivors has ended. If the cause of the crash can be determined, the public will be reassured that similar accidents may be prevented in the future.

Aunt: "She was still a teenager when she met your father. He waited four years to marry her. Supposedly, your father stopped in to see his mother after the first time he saw her and said, 'I just met the girl I'm going to marry.'"

On the radio the announcers are always careful to say, "the so-called black box, or cockpit voice recorder, was recovered." So-called. One announcer explains that the black box, "was located by the" (she pauses) "'pinging' sounds it emits."

Uncle: "Your mother had a hard time in high school. She had a nervous breakdown and dropped out and moved to a commune in Vermont."

One transcript from a cockpit voice recorder includes the voice of an aircraft maintenance engineer speaking to the pilots over the radio. He refused to believe what they were telling him. Damage to the plane had resulted in the loss of all hydraulic systems. The pilots could no longer steer the airplane. The engineer thought this was very unlikely, even impossible. He asked the pilots to verify their loss six times before the plane crashed.

Mother: "The man who did it was an old family friend. He had helped my sister find a job. My parents didn't say anything when I told them. They acted as if nothing had happened. They still invited him over to dinner and let my sister go over there to work in his darkroom. That's when I left home."

My mother has three daughters, but she only told this story to her son.

The black boxes are not black, they are bright orange.

Aunt: "She got her GED in Vermont. Then she went to California for a few years and lived with Liz and Bernie. She worked in a sandwich shop or a Chinese restaurant, I think. One day she just got tired of it and called up Roger to tell him she was ready to marry him. That was it. He came and got her."

She once hitchhiked across the country with truck drivers because she missed her bus in Chicago. She had not needed anyone to come and get her then. Maybe she just got tired of living a life with an unrecognizable shape.

Mother: "Your father taught me how to drive. I had never driven a car before we were married. Our first apartment had a driveway with cement walls. I would scrape the car against the walls almost every time I parked it and I had worn all the paint off one side of the car. Roger and his brother spent a whole weekend sanding it down and repainting it. The day after his brother went back to Syracuse, I scraped it against the wall while I was parking and ruined the new paint job."

My sister admits that she is terrified of making the same mistakes our mother made.

Mother (to herself, from inside her room): "I ruin everything."

I admit to my sister that I don't want to let anyone take care of me.

Grandmother: "Roger must have put her through college. I don't know how he did it, he was still in medical school then. I don't know where she got the money. She never asked us for a dime."

My mother's education includes hours of anatomical drawing of birds from life, the study of fine woodworking and cabinet making with a German master, and a bachelor's degree in English.

Mother: "I couldn't stand his friends from medical school. They were all pompous and awkward. They knew how to memorize but they didn't know how to be human. Rochester was cold and ugly. Everything there was the same color. I was incredibly lonely."

She had her first child that year.

Malcolm McPherson recently collected a book of transcripts from cockpit voice recorders called The Black Box: All-New Cockpit Voice Recorder Accounts of In-Flight Accidents. *It is the updated version of a 1984 "classic." On some of these flights, there were no survivors. Only voices were salvaged.*

Mother: "If your father got his residency in Iowa I would have gone to graduate school there. I was already accepted. He was sent to North Carolina instead."

The transcripts in Malcolm McPherson's book were edited by the National Transportation Safety Board before he published them. Any emotional material was deleted. The curses and apologies that were yelled out just before the crash were deleted. Only material useful to the public in determining the cause of the crash was retained.

Mother: "I'm amazed that more people don't commit suicide. They just keep on living. It's so hard and they just keep doing it."

Useful to the public?

Mother: "Whenever I told him I wanted to work he would tell me that it didn't make any sense. He would say, 'there's no reason for you to work if you'll never be able to make even a fraction of what I make.'"

She hit her thumb with the hammer over and over, nailing wood paneling onto the ceiling of the shed to make a place for me to write. She wanted me to take myself seriously as an artist. Her thumbnail fell off.

All the pilots whose voices are recorded in The Black Box *had extensive training and experience, but many were reluctant to actually fly their planes themselves. The use of autopilot contributed to several crashes. In at least one crash, which resulted in the death of 279 people, the crew might have saved the plane even in the final seconds if they had, "flown the airplane with their own hands."*

Mother: "Rumi wrote that...roughly...the only thing that will be with you to your grave is your work. Only your work will speak for you after you're gone."

There are photographs, as evidence. In every photograph she wears the same strange expression. It's a look I've seen on zoo animals. She had dreams about panthers in cages.

Uncle: "I remember when she visited back then she was like a person living under water. She wandered around like a zombie with you in a basket on her back."

There are only two photos where she seems to be really smiling. Her wedding picture and the formal portrait of her with me, her first child.

Mother: "He used to say that you could lock me in a closet and I'd still get something out of it. I guess that's true."

An investigation of a crash usually also includes the recovery and intensive examination of any debris.

Mother: "I could never keep the house clean. I don't know why."

My sister and I tried to make candles and spilled the hot wax all over the linoleum floor. Our baby brother vomited on the rug.

Aunt: "The place was such a wreck. Your mother was so overwhelmed, she just couldn't keep it clean. You had written all over the walls and burned the table by the time you were two. There were toys everywhere, clothes, dirty dishes in the middle of the floor."

She spent a lot of time in the garden.

Mother: "I felt very...empty."

She also wrote poetry.

Mother: "I did nothing but take care of babies for ten years. Each time one of you stopped being a baby I had another one. I feel like I never got the chance to enjoy any of you as children."

On one of the first days of spring she told me to go outside and lie face down in the clover.

Mother: "I hate to think that there was something I could have done or some kind of drug I could have taken. After spending so much of my life depressed, I hate to think that it didn't have to be that way."

My conversations with my mother consist mostly of silence.

Mother: "..."

There is no way of knowing exactly what the pilots are doing during the silences on the recordings. Reading their instruments? Manipulating the controls? Looking out the window?

Mother (over and over again): "What you have to understand about men is that they aren't like us. They don't have feelings."

My father talks more than my mother, and more easily. But he rarely talks about her.

Father: "One of the things I miss about your mother is the poetry she brought into my life. I still keep a copy of Rumi in the drawer of my desk."

One line of one transcript must have been overlooked by the National Transportation Safety Board. As the plane was going down the pilot said, "Help me hold it. Help me hold it. Help me hold it." The other pilot yelled, "Amy, I love you!"

Mother: "When I started working as a sculptor he told me I was wasting my education. He said, 'I didn't pay for your degree so that you could go off and play with clay.'"

She talks to herself as she hollows out a stoneware bowl. She is saying something about containment. She talks to her dogs and to the chickens. She has said so many things that have gone unheard. Off the record.

Mother: "He made me feel like I wasn't really a writer if I wasn't published. It was as if my poetry didn't mean anything unless it was accepted by someone else."

After the divorce she started her own literary magazine with another woman. She also became a dancer.

One pilot sang a lullaby as his plane went down.

Mother (In an interview for the position of choreographer. She had no experience.): "I have life experience."

THE BALLOONISTS

My father told us stories every night about strange little ani-
mals that came out in the dark. When my father was away, my
mother read us fairy tales that always ended in marriage.
Sometimes, when I missed my father, I slept under my bed in
mourning and the mice crawled all around me.

———

I stand at the window of a bridal shop where huge dresses
hang ghostly in the dark. At the back is a collection of veils
like a row of sleeping jellyfish. One whole wall of the shop is
a mass of white cloth. The wedding dresses are enormous.
They are twice as big as me, and bigger than any woman on
the street.

———

This is the year that everyone is trying to fly around the world
in a balloon. I don't know why.

———

I wonder what my generation will do with what we know of marriage.

I think of a married person as a kind of specialist. It's tempting to have faith in specialists—to assume that barbers know the essential properties of hair and have studied it so thoroughly they can predict exactly how it will fall. But not all barbers are experts or artists or scientists of hair. More often they are just people, not particularly interested in hair, who somehow ended up working with it. One hairdresser mentioned to me, while he cut my hair, that he was considering turning the salon into a burger joint. He wouldn't mind flipping burgers, he said, he just wanted to be doing something with his hands. It's possible, I suppose, that all those married couples are just people, not especially interested in intimacy, who somehow ended up married.

I think it started with model airplanes, the little paper ones. Dad would make complicated adjustments to the wings, the tail, the nose....He would explain everything he was doing while we tried to make grass whistle between our thumbs. Then we would shoot the planes, with rubber bands, off the top of the hill we lived on. If it was a good flight Dad would yell and jump and race after it, and if it crashed he would pick it up and bend the wings a little more.

Then he built a bigger plane, a remote controlled plane. Its wings were as wide as my arm span, and in the first seconds of its first flight it crashed into messy splinters.

I bring home the newspaper for the photos of disasters. Flat, anonymous flood plains are scattered across my floor. Mashed cars with no caption are crumpled in the drawer with my clothes. I tack the thin dribble of wrecked train cars to my wall.

I am beginning to discover everything that I will never be able to do. I realize today, for example, that I will never be a firefighter. I saw an advertisement for firefighters, "no experience necessary," and imagined myself in front of a wall of flame. I would want to watch it burn.

The caption under the picture of the surprised looking little girl reads, "Murder suspect Sylvia Cruz." The article says, "A death that occurs in arson, even if that fire was not intended to cause death, is a homicide."

I can't forget the man on the beach. His tattoo said, "Forgive me Mom."

There are some words that seem to well up from inside me without reason. I will be walking along an empty hallway, leaning against the wall of an elevator, looking at the ceiling of my apartment when I find myself saying, "sorry." But I am not saying it to anyone else, it is only for the sound of the word, the feel of it.

———

All four of us pronounce the word 'sorry' the same way, but different from our parents. Different from anyone that lives around us. There is no explaining it.

———

In my dream we are all waiting for my sister. The sails on the boat are stretching out over the lake, huge and full. She comes late. What's wrong? She's gotten married accidentally. God, Mavis, how could that happen? Dad is angry, we are all crying. I wake up afraid that she will be taken and folded up in a closet like clean linen.

———

Walking home with four bags of groceries I fell on the asphalt. Apples bounced out of the bags, bruising. When it was dark and the groceries were all put away, I undressed to find that my knees were split open and my legs were crusted with dried blood. I hadn't felt anything.

———

The cuts were closed by the time I slept in his bed for the first time. He ran his finger along my side, gently, over my hip. My knees stung, my wrists hurt, my head was pounding, and everything tickled.

I am in the car. Peaches floating in a mason jar. The slant of the early sun is sharp. The glass of the window is too thin and through it everything looks jagged. A lone pumpkin sits on the highway. Behind it a smokestack rises gracefully, thin and burnt. We are at a stoplight and tape from a cassette is glistening and twisting on the road. Sinking and blowing and catching under tires without a sound.

I feel his hand, through a red glove, on my leg. There are boats out there under covers, all different colors.

—

My father built a canoe with his father. It was like a wingless airplane made of wood. He started making another one by himself that sat for years, a skeleton on braces, in various stages of incompletion. "When I finish my canoe" was the beginning of so many of my father's sentences. He talked about the boats he would build the way some people talk about the money they will make. As if it were all he needed.

—

I was crying, or trying to cry, sitting on a folding metal chair in the first row. Grandma, behind me, was definitely crying. What Dad didn't know is that while he was saying his vows we were watching a cloud of black smoke rising in the window behind him. It hung there like a sleeping whale. Did he notice the smell of burning rubber as we got into the car to leave? All his little girls dressed in white and his fidgety son, twisting our heads to see the smoke hanging over the Colonie town dump. I think I remember him saying that the problem with a tire fire is that it can smolder for years, burning quietly but uncontrollably.

—

My father holds the tips of his fingers together to show the shape of the boat he wants to build. He will use two types of wood, for their strength, and because a light color will be beautiful against rose. It will be outfitted in brass and the sails will cut across each other like wings opening.

—

I have almost no memory of my mother from the time before the divorce. It is as if she did not exist until I was nine. I remember that we used to climb on Dad and ask over and over, "Where's Mom? Where's Mommy?" And he used to say, "Down a hole."

—

The couple on the train are young. She is wearing high heels and he has on a suit. She is staring straight ahead, and he is staring at the dark window where he probably sees his own reflection. She absently touches her index finger to his, over and over.

—

I fall asleep fast and wake up without a sense of time, knowing only that I feel his fingers around my waist, his mouth on my stomach. I ask him what he has been doing while I slept. "I've been kissing your belly."

—

I watched him play across a crowded concert hall with a high ceiling. I was late, so I sat in the aisle, directly in front of him. He bent into the drums and looked straight at me. I stared back and blushed. He winced, I was riveted, captivated, possessed.

—

Later, he asked if I had been there.

—

In the subway I see a couple dancing salsa for money. He is spinning her in a red blur. I worry about how close her head is coming to the wall, but she is loose and unconcerned. Her hair is flying and her skirt is coming up. She pays no attention. He stops spinning her and I am amazed at how close they dance, how her feet seem attached to his at the toes. His face is ecstatic, sweat-beaded, eyes turned upwards. He must be in love. But there is something strange about the woman, I realize, something strange about the way she's moving. They turn and I see that her face is plastic, her arms are tied around his neck, her feet are attached to his at the toes, her legs are foam. He controls her movements with his hands inside her hips. His eyes are closed.

I think I remember the sound of my mother typing in the basement. But this is only because I know there was a typewriter down there. I don't know how much she used it. She was almost always home, but if she wasn't typing and she wasn't in the garden and she wasn't putting bread in the oven, what was she doing?

I'm standing right in front, watching the drummer, as if by studying him I could learn some secret about all drummers. This man's hair is gray and he holds the sticks effortlessly. He is barely touching them, they just happen to be inside his hands. A squished-face man steps in front of me and yells to the drummer, "Hey Ronny." No response. He sees me notice him and says, "See, me and my man Ron go way back, and that man loves him some music. Loves that music. He gonna marry him some music he love it so bad."

My father played the trumpet every evening. He played taps out across the river. He played his banjo even though we always tried to pluck on the strings while he held it. He sang. Even after the divorce, he sang every time we were in a boat.

———

A man is hurrying down the street with a little girl hanging on his hand. She is dragging, tripping a little and he looks down as if he has just noticed her, saying, "I'm sorry sweetheart," and lifting her to his shoulders.

———

"How is your father?" my grandmother asks. "You know, I loved Roger and now I feel as if he has died. I haven't talked to him in years...."

———

"Your mom had to leave him or she wouldn't have survived. I'm not sure why. When I think of her with that garden, and you four kids, and that old man in the extra room who was always sick....You know, she used to tear down parts of that house and put them back together herself."

———

"There are so many different kinds of wrecking bars in use that it would be difficult to present them all. The wrecking bar is called by different names. The crowbar is also called a pinch bar. A wrecking bar with a slightly bent chisel point on one end and a hook with claws on it is also called a gooseneck bar and, frequently, a ripping bar."
—*Carpenter's Tools*, H. H. Siegele

———

I like to think that the house was hollower after my mother left, but it just sounded that way because of the piano. Dad bought a pea-green piano and took it apart, scraped the paint piece by piece, sanded it, stained it, varnished it layer by layer, and then put it back together several times until it worked.

———

We wake up to the sound of the neighbor singing, "The thrill is gone..." The air is cool and the shade is glowing. His hand is cupped over the back of my neck. My face is against his chest, my leg is thrown over his stomach. I fall asleep and when I wake up again we are holding each other's faces, noses touching.

—

One pedal on the piano squeaks.

—

My father learned to sail from reading books. He studied diagrams of the wind, alone in the evenings after my mother left. I lay in bed listening to the pages turn in the kitchen.

—

I am staring at the map, the wide winding patterns, the tangle, the mess. He understands it. He wonders about breaks and pauses in the vibration patterns on the water. I wonder about the pipes and rivets rusted into the walls of the canal. The mossy spigots, the empty mechanisms, the lock grown over with blackberries.

—

"Sandy was a horrible woman," my mother tells me, "but Ed loved her, and when she married him something about her changed. Maybe it was the security, or the love, but she softened. They had a little plane, one of those frail, noisy ones, and they used to go flying together all the time. Then Ed crashed it and died. That really destroyed Sandy, she was intolerable after that."

—

My Dad has always been waiting for a day with the right wind.

The kites he liked had two or three strings, stunt kites that would spin and swirl. We would go to the top of every hill around and it was always raining or very cold. The four of us would huddle together, fighting a little, while Dad assembled the kite and laid out the strings and ran crazily until it finally took off. There would be a staccato series of nose-dives, but he didn't give up easy.

———

There are so many things that make me sad. Kite strings, oatmeal, the white walls and the fan rushing, the tan plastic blinds, my dream about climbing on houses like these and breaking them.

———

Carrying the kite that had hung on his wall for a year, we walked back to the elementary school where I had been in sixth grade when he was in fifth. The playground equipment was not where it used to be. The kite went up easily. I was singing, "You look like rain..." We took turns letting out string, it had a powerful pull, the weight of the wind was strange to hold. The kite was the size of a bird dipping down. We let out another spool of string. It was the size of a blinking airplane in the dusk. We let out a third spool. All that string was hanging in the air, softly suspended. We imagined that pulling the string made the kite move minutes later. He put his arms around my stomach and the last of the string zipped off the spool. I watched the end float lightly up into the air. It dissolved as he ran after it. Three spools of string and a kite swallowed into the evening. He stood in the middle of the field. "You lost my kite!"

———

*A friend of mine served jury duty on a traffic vio-
lation case in which a young man had rear-ended
an elderly woman who was driving the speed
limit. The woman was very sweet and timid—
her hands shook. What made the case difficult was
the man's defense. He admitted that he hadn't
been paying attention to the speed limit. "I was
rushing home to see my beautiful wife." He had
been out of town and hadn't seen her for days. He
had been speeding. He was a handsome young
man with a beautiful wife. The jury found him
not guilty.*

When I was six a boy named Brent asked me to marry him. He was my babysitter's son. His brother listened to *The Chipmunks' Christmas Album* while we dug pennies out of the soft moldy couch where he would lie on top of me with sticky lips against my ear saying, "Let's make love."

—

I used to put on a skirt to work in the restaurant where the waiter, Jimmy, would slip up behind me and slide a jar of sugar packets into my hand. A sudden cool weight in my palm. The bartender brought me a cherry on a toothpick, wrapped in a napkin. Later he brought me two, and I had to touch his hand to take them. Juan, the busboy, smiled a strange, soft smile and whispered, "Como estas?" The man in the first seat of the bus just hissed, a low hiss.

—

The supermarket is too bright, and the ceiling is too high. I'm watching the man in front of me in line. He turns his head to glance back at me every few seconds and I look away. He has brownish stains at the corners of his mouth. He is rubbing his thumb over his other thumbnail, nervously. His fingers are stained.

—

My father was coming home from a trip and I wanted to get the polish off my nails. I didn't know yet how to get it off and I couldn't wait, so I stood over the sink carefully scraping it away with my jackknife.

—

He likes to stretch out his hands in mine so that I can see the red marks between his fingers, where he holds the sticks, and the knobs of calluses where he has no feeling. I am always aware of his hands. They are long and knuckled, with the smoothest brown skin. They smell like soap. "I'm afraid something will happen to my hands," he says, "I need my hands."

—

The way he touches an instrument, a mixing bowl, the door-knob, is so gentle. He is someone who believes he can break things, or he believes that anything can hurt him.

———

When he was eight he kept a diary pressed under his mattress. He carefully wrote believable details in it each day. Details like, "Mom made cookies," "The dog next door bit the boy that lives there," "I fell off my bike." What he wrote had the same texture as his life, but it was never true. That way, if someone came into his room, lifted the mattress, and opened the book, they still wouldn't know anything about him. Eventually, not even that was enough. He took the notebook into the woods and burned it, leaving the wire spiral to rust.

———

The wind is blowing through my apartment and I hear geese, I think, and maybe thunder. Now the wind is still and I hear a hubcap fall off a car.

———

He thinks I don't pay attention. He has been talking and I have been silently naming the scents of everything we are crushing under our feet as we walk.

———

He used to have headaches that made him vomit. Nothing would make them go away. His doctor made him hold a thermometer and concentrate on raising his body temperature one degree at a time. His headaches were worse when his mother was in the room.

———

We undress in the little room which the heater is just begin-ning to warm. Bugs are coming alive. He is under the blankets and there are three wasps on the ceiling. He says he can't sleep knowing they are there. In my underwear, I roll up a magazine and stand on a chair to hit the wasps.

29

I was drinking tea with his mother while he cut ice off the roof with a shovel. He hurt himself, somehow, and came in the door suddenly, furious, splattering snow all over the room. He sat on the couch and stared straight ahead, just breathing. His mother and I stopped talking, kept drinking our tea.

———

He grew up on short streets that ended in yield signs or dead ends. Lighters were fascinating. Sometimes his older brother made fires in the back yard.

———

He wanted to change his image. He was only ten but he had been depressed and his mother was worried. She took him shopping for new clothes and told him he could get anything he wanted. He picked neon colors, diagonal stripes and all the patterns that made his eyes hurt. He was very shy and he looked completely absurd. This is what he wanted. He says that after he got his new clothes it was easier for him to go to school.

———

In his room the shades are pulled down so the windows glow pearly like projections on blank screens. The springs of a folded bed, the sharp cymbals of his drum set, the mallets and bars of the vibraphone all make a sharp nest around his bed. His blankets smell of dust and sweat. There is a mat of sheet music, books, and underwear on the floor. It is sprinkled with sand spilled from the jar that John West brought back from Bermuda in third grade.

———

He touches my hair and says, "If we were my parents, we would be getting married now, do you know that?"

———

"Sonata," he says, "means 'sounding together.' It is an argument in which one theme is presented in opposition to another and they struggle until one wins, in the resolution. It is a beautiful form, it has endured into this century."

———

I'm trying to explain something to him and he cuts off my last word to say, "Let's go in." So I slam the car door and he sighs. Sitting at the bar in the diner, with our legs dangling off the stools, we can't look at each other and we can't look at the truckers, the teenagers in booths, or up at the waitress. His cup of coffee sits in front of him and he can't pick it up. I finger my place mat and can't say anything. I move to get up, but he catches my arm, still not looking at me, and says, "We came all the way here, now let's enjoy it."

———

There is a woman who has a little table full of alarm clocks in front of the building where I work. She stands there with a vacant face while people walk by and one of the alarms goes off endlessly.

———

"Never marry a musician on New Year's Eve," is his mother's advice to me. "You'll always spend your anniversary alone." I can hardly hear her over the music. Her husband and her son are on stage, and we are standing awkwardly in a room full of glittery people. We stand there until midnight, after the countdown, when we go up to the stage to get our kisses and come back to stand by the dessert table. "You should have seen Charlie," she says to me, leaning over and pointing to her husband, conspiratorial, giggling a little. "That woman in the tiny little gold dress came over and asked to borrow a chair, she leaned down and his mouth just fell open. He sat there and stared at her until he realized what was going on and said 'Oh, yeah, yeah, sure.'"

On my way down the fire escape in the rain I see a boy flop down on his bed. Through the curtains I see only his stomach and arms, which are still for a second until his hand reaches for his guitar, drawing it over his chest.

—

My grandmother signs the letter with both their names. In it she admits that she doesn't know if her husband is happy.

—

I come home to an empty house and fill the sink with water. The pigeons above the window are clucking. I let the dishes slip under the bubbles and I close my eyes. I listen to the perfect, whole, round sounds of glass against porcelain under water.

—

He hears his mother and his sister-in-law talk about how lonely it is to be married to a musician, how many nights they spend alone. He wonders if I would be unhappy. I don't say anything. I like to spend my nights alone.

—

"We tell ourselves stories in order to live," writes Joan Didion, with a certain skepticism. We also live by the stories we tell. It is enough for the end of a fairy tale to read simply, "...then they were married." I suspect my father, among others, of marrying in order to locate himself within this kind of easy fairy tale. I do not doubt that he loved my mother, but I do know that he deliberately looked for a wife. My father has told me more than once that although he doesn't think his parents did everything right, he hasn't had much else to model the shape of his life after.

"I was married in the same suit I graduated high school in," my father says. "I didn't go to my college graduation, but it was also the same suit I graduated medical school in. It wasn't even my suit, it was a hand-me-down from my brother Lynn."

—

"Try not to argue," my father says quietly, putting his hand on my shoulder after I yell into the phone and hang up loudly.

—

My mother is telling me about the *Oprah* she saw on couples who never should have been married. "The strange thing about it," she says, "is that most of them knew even before they got married that it would never work, but something made them do it anyway."

—

I was standing in the bathroom of the house my mother was renting. I was opening the little dark wooden box that had held my mother's wedding ring for so long. This was my ritual. I would take it out of the box and try it on my finger, turn it over and over. I would imagine myself in a white dress. "I do." But it wasn't in the box, and neither was the one that Dad had given back to her. "Mom," I was standing on a stool, teetering a little, "Mommy, your wedding ring is gone." She came to the doorway and looked at me. "I don't have it anymore, honey." She turned and walked into the kitchen, saying "I threw it in the lake. Your father loved water."

—

When we all slept in the same bed, my mother used to tell me that Dad and I talked to each other in our sleep. My mother offered to pay me a dollar for every week I slept in my own bed.

—

On the Fourth of July my father and I used to sit on the back porch and watch the fireworks across the river. They were tiny flares on the edge of the sky, we would miss them if we were looking in the wrong place. So we leaned forward, waiting, and we shouted when we saw one. Dad would judge by the direction which town it was coming from, and he would map out the area beyond the river with his hands.

———

I remember piling all the furniture in my room against the door because I knew I had done something bad. I remember dashing up the stairs and quickly choosing a book from the shelf to put in the back of my pants to protect me. My mother remembers standing at the picture window, watching my father chase me around and around the house.

———

I am sitting on a rock taking pictures of my father. It may be the same rock that my mother sat on when she took the pictures in the photo album that is lost now. But he isn't thinking of this. For him, everything is the waves and his muscles. He braces the paddle and then the boat is motionless on the river with the foam crashing all around it.

He understands the nature of water. He talks about it with words like 'eddy,' 'flume,' 'hole,' 'rapid'.... He knows about the strange force of it, the suction, the press, the grasp, the airlessness of it. And he loves it.

I swim against the current and he paddles over to point out the rocks for me. I swim as hard as I can, going nowhere. I notice that his hair is all gray now.

———

My father named his first sailboat after his second wife. "Cathy's Clown." "That's stupid," my mother muttered when she heard about it, "Has he listened to the words of that song? It's like getting a license plate that says, 'accident.'"

———

He has been reading the 1996 almanac like a novel. He is in the disaster section now. "Notable Floods, Notable Fires, Notable Earthquakes...."

———

My mother knows how to sharpen several different kinds of blades. She was an apprentice to a master carpenter after she left high school. She still has some of his tools. When I left home, I took a book from her shelf, *Carpenter's Tools*, by H. H. Siegele. It is bound in soft red cloth, and some of the sections are repeated or in the wrong order.

———

The flower pot that I broke was a wedding gift to my mother from a woman with a heart condition that made her so weak she had to stay in bed. Her husband needed to take care of her, and when they asked her if she wanted to risk the operation she said yes. During the operation she died.

———

My mother was very sick and my father had a dream that she died. He told her that at first in the dream he was sad, and then he just felt excited. She says this is when she knew she had to leave him.

———

My mother had a dream that my father was driving a rusty old pickup in the rain, going too fast and sliding all over. He was coming towards her, where she was standing with his dead father, and his father said to her, pulling her away, "Watch out, he is crazy." He was sad, shaking his head. My mother says this is when she knew she had to leave him.

———

My mother went to Arizona with another man. A poet. I don't know what she told my father. She didn't dream about him. I think this is when she knew she had to leave him.

———

I got out of bed because I heard something downstairs, in the dark. It was whimpering and sniffling and choking. It was my mother crying in the rocking chair. I climbed up on her lap and tried to peel her fingers off her face. "Why are you crying, Mom?" She was quiet for a long time. "Because your father wants me to do something I can't do." "What is it?" "He said that if I never see Carl again, if I say I don't love Carl, he will forget about everything that has happened." It sounded like a fair deal. "Why don't you do it, Mom?" She cried harder.

———

He was soft to me at first, but after I told him he wrestled away from me and slammed the door. I was left with the open window, the rain sounds, and his bags on my floor. He came back and wouldn't be near me, wouldn't let me touch him. My stomach hurt. Finally he cried and shook. He didn't say anything. We slept sweetly.

———

There are marks left by paint on my hands, my fingernails, the hairs of my arm. Marks on my palm, one for each place that grips the shovel. A mark on my hip where the knife in my pocket rubs against the bone. A strip of burn on my back from bending in the sun.

———

That place, low on my back, that I might not have noticed if it was not burning. That I might not have noticed if my mother hadn't bent over the potatoes with her back to the house so many times that a crescent of pale skin is marked on my memory.

———

I am sewing in the sun. There are so many black threads lost in the grass. My mother said sewing was one of the things that she knew she should like to do but hated. This bothered her all the time, and sometimes she would sit down and try very hard to sew something. My father taught me to sew. It was the quilting stitch he used to fix the spray skirt on his kayak.

———

When I get into the car, my mother is tying a thin string around a brown box with a coffee cake inside. I keep thinking about that string, wound around so many times but still a bit loose, tied with a too-long bow.

———

Letter: "If we lived together, we would have deep red curtains, like in your room at home. But no plastic shades. Or, maybe we would have those shades but I would always be rolling them up and you would always be pulling them down and eventually they would break.... I might not send this letter."

———

My littlest sister is telling me about her birthday party. She turned thirteen this year. One of the best parts, she said, was that when the elevator stopped to pick them up, a bride and her bridesmaids were inside. She was perfect, my sister squealed, the perfect bride, she was so beautiful, and her dress was so beautiful. "We all said, 'Aaahhh.'"

———

Words like 'custody' don't mean the same thing to him. I don't want us to own anything together. "You don't want to be happy," he accuses me.

———

Are we going to keep living the same stories our parents lived?

I played with moss during that time. There is a lichen called famine bread. My father's pancakes were out in the snow for the birds. One night we ate at McDonald's, one night we ate at Taco Bell, two nights we had spaghetti, and every once in a while we had cube steak cooked forever with vegetables and potatoes that came from a box. The neighbors said it was a shame. Dad put soap on the table and made huge bubbles with his hands.

—

My mother was in the bathtub crying and I was standing outside the door waiting, just in case she decided to slip her head under and keep it there. The other kids were upstairs. The problem was about money, of course. She was afraid she wouldn't have enough for us to eat.

—

There is a blind accordion player on the Number 6 train. He opens the door of the car, stumbling, and then stands for a minute swaying until he begins to play. He plays and walks very slowly down the length of the car, bumping into every pole unless a hand reaches out to guide him past it. He does this down the whole length of the train, over and over, every day.

—

My mother makes pumpkin pies from no recipe. Gutting the pumpkin, cutting it into chunks, cooking it in a cast-iron pot, checking the stove. Sometimes pumpkin pie for lunch and dinner, sometimes pumpkin soup. She brings in the buckets of potatoes, she lines up all the new eggs by the sink and washes them gently. She is so thin that her ribs are deep ridges. Sometimes, she tells me, she remembers and makes up for it by eating some butter.

—

My aunt lays out the silverware and my uncle comes in and sits at the table. For him there is fresh bread, salad, baked potatoes, and corned beef. She eats a bowl of rice. My grandmother calls it her "problem."

—

I was shaking when I asked my mother, "Do you think you eat enough?" She was silent for a long time until she said quietly, "That is between me and God."

—

A huge metal pipe brings the stream under the road and out into the river. I remember exactly the echoes it made when we threw rocks up against its side. The pipe is less round now. I'm standing on the railroad bridge that we used to climb under. The boys always dared me to jump from the iron supports. I thought about it, weighing my chances given the length of the fall and the depth of the water.

—

I was reading my mother's poems, all at once. When I finished I walked into the kitchen and opened a cupboard where a jar of vanilla extract fell onto my head and broke, stinging my eyes. I drove away on slippery dark roads over the mountains, still smelling of vanilla. I was afraid, and there were no radio stations.

—

I bent over, sick, and leaned my head against the softness of his stomach. He wrapped his arms around me, rocking gently. He said, "We should take you to the ocean, maybe that's what you need to feel better."

—

He sang into my ear, under his breath. Silly songs. "That's the recipe for making love..."

—

Mom and I take turns with the saw, slicing into the red center of a cedar root. I am only visiting. She wears socks on her hands to keep them warm.

—

My mother's poems were in a faded blue binder. Some were yellowed, some had bent corners, some had notes penciled at the bottom. They were not in the order in which they were written.

She wrote about my father ice skating, she wrote about me, in the bow of a boat, scared by an owl and crying for the moon to fill the water. She wrote about nursing until she had no more milk. She wrote lovingly of potatoes.

—

When my mother first brought us to her new house we hadn't seen her for a long time. The house had a swing set, and she asked us, "What do you think, do you like it?" And I said, "It is very square."

—

On the first Thanksgiving at my mother's house I was yelling because I wanted everyone to dress up and they wouldn't. You have to dress up on Thanksgiving, and you have to have a turkey, you should also say grace. I was crying. We didn't have a turkey but we had soup. Mom had spilled a box of paper clips into the soup and we kept picking them out and laying them on our napkins.

—

Dissertations have been written on The Effect of Parental Alienation Syndrome. *Doctoral candidates have measured children of divorce on the "Happiness Index." There have been studies using the "Family Adaptability and Cohesion Scale" and the "Adjustment Scale." But there has been no measure of the level of disillusionment with the standard story. There is no "Trust in Narrative Scale". There has been no study of the undercurrents of disbelief running through our lives. What if an entire generation were to reject their central story line?*

The instrument cases. Snare, bass, cymbals— all in black cases. Taking up the whole living room. Stacked by the door, ready to be loaded. Fitted into the trunk of the car. In the back of a bar, filling up with smoke. On the stage after he has finished playing.

—

They are all black, all plain and boxy. Some have velvet inside. I like to close them. Mute casings. They have silver latches. They are so quiet that they can crowd a room without being noticed. I sat on one to eat oatmeal, without realizing that it was there. He backed over one in his car. They are not fragile.

—

The bag of groceries has been jabbing my leg all the way home. I can't find the frying pan and I'm getting angry, stamping on the floor. I find it in a cabinet above my head and pull on the handle, "Get down here." All the pans fall, hitting me on the head, bouncing off the stove, denting the door behind me, and clanging on the floor. I sit on the couch crying into my hands. I realize that I also sat this way yesterday. I was in a different city, and a different house. Without thinking and for no reason, I stuck out my foot to trip him at the top of the stairs. He stumbled and caught the railing, saying something sharp. I went into the bathroom and sat on the closed toilet, crying into my hands. I could hear him in the doorway. "Honey...." I didn't look up. I listened to him walk down the stairs and start washing the dishes.

—

"We are not close," he said, and let the effect linger before he said, "We live five hundred miles apart."

—

I was walking in the dark and a car that had just passed me slowed down and began backing up. Someone leaned out the

44

passenger's side and looked back at me. A voice from inside the car asked something and the person leaning out said, "No, it isn't," and rolled the window back up. They drove away and I kept walking.

—

Black is closing in around my eyes. I realize with a great, tired sadness that I am losing the world. The walls, the molding on the door frame, the yellow of the lamp, his back at the sink… are all achingly beautiful. I reach out and feel myself groping in the air, feel myself falling great distances, feel nothing at all. Suddenly, with a red rush I can breathe and I can see. I get up from the floor before he turns around and says, "You look flushed."

—

I'm tired of the highway and the slow numbers on my odometer. When the gas tank light comes on for the second time I still haven't spoken to anyone all day.

—

I pause when the man at the register lays down a red carnation with my change, says quietly, "This is for you," and turns to the next customer. As I am starting my car I see another woman smiling and stepping into her car, holding a white carnation.

—

He is leaving, again. On the way to the station we pass an accident, broken glass all over the street and a policeman directing traffic. A big box of Kleenex is lying next to the curb with one tissue pulled out, fluttering in the wind. I kiss him through the gate of the subway and he smiles sweetly, sheepishly. On my way home the box of Kleenex is still there. I stand by the bed, looking over the white sheets. All day there has been hammering and screwdriving upstairs. I can hear little girls giggling through the window. I shake out the sheets and make the bed. I put the couch back together.

—

My sister tells me that her boyfriend asked her, over the phone, if she thought they would ever get married. It was late and the other kids had gone to bed. There was a breeze coming through her window. She pulled up the pink rosebud comforter and crickets whispered through the walls. "I don't know," she said, "Do you?" "I don't know," he answered, "do you want to?" "I don't know," she said, "do you?" He didn't know.

—

His parents are still married. His father watches TV when he isn't working. His mother volunteers at the church and takes cookies to the neighbors.

—

His brother is thinking about having a baby. He got married four years ago and bought a house. We visited them there and watched the wedding video. They are both teachers and they have a big deck by the lake.

—

There is a TV show called "A Wedding Story," where they interview a loving couple and show all the preparations for the wedding — sending out the invitations, buying the cake, putting on the dress and, finally, the kiss. The next show after "A Wedding Story" is called "A Baby Story."

—

I move one seat closer to the couple on the bus. They are holding hands but she is looking out her window and he is looking at his lap. They don't seem to be mad at each other.

—

My parents have not talked to each other for more than five years. They occasionally send notes. Mom says, "Tell your father...." Once I went to a concert with my mother and my father was there. In the same room. They had four children together.

"We drove past our old house," the woman told me, "and I noticed that the tree he had watered through the droughts and cared for over the years had been cut down. He must have noticed too. I didn't say anything. I thought, 'I won't talk about it until he does,' but he didn't say a word."

He held up the map between us, so that the light shone through it, the roads on one side knotting with the roads on the other. His hand was a shadow on the web. He pressed his thumb on one point: "This is me." His index finger brushed another point: "This is you." He lifted his hand so that I could see the distance.

Today I noticed a slim bar of soap lodged deep in the throat of the sink. My fingers can't reach that far down the drain. It is leaching away into the water, every day.

I see his toothbrush in its case and I want to cover it with a towel. The plastic is too much like secret pillboxes, the shape too much like an unfinished toy, the shade of pink too much like something from inside the body. It is like finding his ear after pushing away so much black hair. Mute, sleeping in its own tunnels. An internal organ curled in the shape of a little fetus on the side of his head. I want to fold it tenderly and tuck it back in.

When he tells me to stop for the red light I slap his leg angrily as I am braking. My hand stings a little and he won't speak to me for the rest of the trip.

On the day Martha died, she came into the room where Joan was still sleeping and said, "I have a terrible headache and it's all your fault." Then she went into the garage and slammed her hand in the car door. She came back and asked Joan to

47

take her to the hospital, but Joan was still in bed and told her to get someone else to take her. While Martha was at the hospital she died of a massive stroke. Martha left everything to Joan, and Joan left town as soon as she could. Mom says, "Joan was awful to Martha, but in the end, Martha got her back."

———

I asked him for a bedtime story. I didn't really want a story, I just wanted him to talk to me. He couldn't think of anything. When I woke up he was gone but there was a letter on my bed that began, "So, you wanted a bedtime story…."

———

In the subway I fell asleep on his lap with his hand under my face. I felt dizzy when our stop came, stumbled up the steps, and stumbled all the way to my apartment. He said, "Do you want me to carry you? I will."

———

Later, maybe in bed, he told me, "You looked so terrible when you woke up. One side of your face was pale white, the other was bright red with the pattern of my hand pressed into it. I was worried about you."

———

Then he admitted, "While you were sleeping I thought about getting off at our stop without you. You would wake up in Harlem or the Bronx and I would be gone and you wouldn't know where you were. You'd be sleepy and confused and alone."

———

The cockpit voice recorder from Tuesday's crash has been found. I want to know what the two pilots in the cockpit were saying to each other as "a series of vital operating systems on the plane was gradually breaking down."

———

48

My father's second wife, my stepmother, moved with her daughter to a new house a few miles away from where she lived with my father. She took the stereo, a couch, some pictures, all the silverware, and the dog. She left the quilts on the walls, the ducks with bows, the wallpaper she had picked out, and boxes in the basement.

Sometimes my stepmother came back to make dinner and left after doing the dishes. She came back to plant bulbs in the back yard and she came back to cook Thanksgiving dinner. My father's family didn't know that she had left. She came back for Christmas Day.

———

After my stepmother took the couch, my father put a Ping-Pong table in its place. We all played Ping-Pong and laughed until it was time to go to bed. When she started to come back every night, the Ping-Pong table got folded up and put in the garage.

———

When my stepmother left again, the pots that she used to fill with tight little flowers got brown and mossy. For my sister's graduation party she came back to the house and ordered lasagna. She put flowers in the pots and let her dog run around everyone's legs.

———

I was twenty before Dad taught me to use the chainsaw. My memories of fall days are full of its sound and smell.

Now it breathes oily smoke up my shirt. I wince, chips fly. I would rather pick up logs and toss them. But the machine is so compact, red, muscular.

In the car, with the chainsaw in the trunk, my father tells me that his wife has left for the third time. The final time, he thinks. He wonders if he is too selfish to be a good husband. Dad. He says something about his childhood, he can't stop living it. Dad. I think he may be wiping away tears, but I don't look.

Things with her, he says, were a disaster in slow motion.

—

I touch the panes of glass in his window as I look out at the snow. My mother wrote many winter poems. She gets cold too easily, like me. Our hands don't get enough blood. The first winter that she lived with my father he bought her a new pair of mittens almost every day. He tried wool, and rabbit fur, and thermal mesh. Nothing kept her warm.

—

We are riding in the car at night, in the rain, and I tell him what my father told me about pilots in World War II. Instrument panels were new to them, and sometimes hard to believe. Pilots in a downward spiral wouldn't feel anything, and if it was dark enough wouldn't see the horizon, so they often ignored the needles spinning on their dials.

—

I walked away from his house bareheaded, in the middle of the night. The snow was sucking up all the sound, so there was only the steady whine of transformers on the telephone poles. The sky was milky and the streetlights made a soft eerie trail down the empty road. I stood in the middle of the intersection, directly under the traffic light. It swayed slightly above me, and I was suddenly impressed with its weight. It was a huge black box suspended in the air, a ghostly metal body. As the colors changed, it clicked. The air filled thickly with orange. A tunnel of snow was illuminated. I stood beneath the box as it signaled relentlessly.

—

"At some point," my mother tells me, "you realize that your parents are not who you thought they were. You realize that they are something separate from what you have made out of them." She tells me this because she knows I have been writing about her. It is what she says instead of saying, "You don't know me."

"For example," she says, "my sister always felt that our father didn't like her. Of course he liked her, he just didn't understand how to show that he liked her. She didn't really have a father that didn't like her, but that doesn't change the fact that she had the experience of having a father who didn't like her." My mother is telling me that I am not a liar, but that she is not what I write about her.

The bus was stopped at a light and the old man leaned across the aisle to his wife.

"Where did we come from?"

"Syracuse," she said sharply. She had bright lipstick. He swallowed and looked away. He spoke more slowly.

"Where did we come from?"

"What do you mean? 712 Milton Ave, Syracuse."

He shook his head.

"No, where did we come from." His voice was more urgent, but still low.

"Milton Ave, Jim," she said without looking at him. He stared at the seat in front of him, gathering himself. Turning to her, holding out his bus ticket, his hand shaking slightly, he said,

"Originally. Originally, where did we come from?"

"Syracuse."

He shook his head.

"Can't you think of anywhere else we might have come from?"

She looked at him, pausing.

"Not that I remember, Jim, no."

He stared at the seat in front of him again.

"I have the feeling we've done this before," he mumbled under his breath. He glanced at the woman, looked away, and glanced back. She didn't meet his eyes.

Where are we going?" he asked.

She didn't smile. "Rochester."

He slapped his knee and leaned closer to her. "Yeah, now we're talking, now we're talking. Okay, Rochester, now, after that, if you had to go on, where would you go?"

—

His parents were married when they were eighteen and nineteen. His father played for the army band and his mother followed behind their bus in her Volkswagen.

—

He wants me to move to Rochester to be with him.

—

I don't know where my parents met. I don't know where they were married. I know that they lived in Rochester at first. I know that I was born there. There is a picture of my mother holding me, wearing her graduation gown. She was in her last year of college. I know that she hated it there. That she only stayed because of my father. I know that my father's bike was stolen more than once. I know that she believes she could have been a writer if she had taken her chance and left. My father still talks about his green racing bike, the one he put together himself.

—

We are still sitting in the parking lot. There is rain on the windshield. Big globe lights wobble through the droplets and I watch the patterns of light running over his face. I want to go to bed. Fine. He starts the car and drives all the way home without speaking. I am groping for the door handle when he says, "Everything you do costs... something."

—

One whole side of his body grew too fast, so that he had to have part of his leg cut out. There is a long scar across his knee from it. My father has the same scar, from crashing his motorcycle at night on a wet bridge.

—

There is a water tower on a hill in the town where we grew up. It is painted red and white now, but when it was new it was gray. He tells me that he went inside the water tower when it was still gray and new, before it was filled with water. He walked there through the woods and when he stepped inside he could hear the echoes of his breath. He clapped his hands together once and the echoes came back at him from every direction, overlapping and shuddering against each other. It was like being caught in a flock of birds. He picked up a piece of pipe from the floor. He says he can almost still feel the reverberation in his chest every time he drives past the water tower.

—

It is winter and his nose begins to bleed as he bends over the sink splashing water onto his closed eyes. When he looks into the mirror his face is covered in blood.

—

I don't know why they let me keep the mourning dove after the cat caught it. I put it in my room and whispered to it, tried to push bread into its beak and cover its one ruined eye with a Band-Aid. It stood there and shivered until it fell over.

—

He called to tell me that his nose wouldn't stop bleeding. He went from one hospital to another until, in the hospital where I was born, they cauterized him so his nose would never bleed again.

———

The sound of a shade going up scares me. When my father talks about the time after he was first married, he talks about the rivers he raced canoes on. My mother mentioned, only once, how lonely she was.

———

Getting off a Greyhound bus, I return for the first time to the city where I was born. I am the age that my mother was then. I look out his window across a morning where the entire city is brown except for a Newport billboard on top of a paint factory. "Alive With Pleasure!" I think about my mother while I watch him play at the concert hall. And I think of her while I stand at the window with my back to him where he sits with his bathrobe open and we argue about how long I will stay.

———

As we stand waiting for our drinks, his thumb plucks my spine in time with the bass in the music. At night, when he absently presses my side like the keys on a piano, he is not being tender so much as he is working out a problem.

———

When he says, "Why can't you follow a recipe?" I am hurt, because I know that he is not just asking why I can't be told what to do, but also why I can't let things be simple.

———

There is a picture of a balloon in the newspaper again today. "Steve Fossett and his silvery balloon made it more than 7,000 miles this time, from St. Louis to Southern Russia. But his equipment was failing. The wind was hostile. And he was slowly freezing." I turn the page, satisfied.

———

Both of the times I came close to drowning, I was with my father. The first time, the boat flipped over and a rope caught my foot. For a few seconds I was held under in a tangle of panic and metal and rope. When I came up, no one had noticed and I never mentioned it.

The second time, he asked me, "Can you pull this?" The release loop was tight, but I thought if I was drowning I would be able to pull anything. Upside down, pushed against a rock with water rushing all around my head, I could not reach the loop. It was dark and I was trapped in the boat and I wasn't sure where to search for the surface. My father dragged me out. I was shaking and he was white in the face. We joke about it now.

———

The laws of water are very difficult. No matter how many times it is explained to me, I don't understand how the tides work. I know, of course, that water will seek a level. I know that it will only flow down.

———

I grew up by the Hudson, the river that flows both ways. Where I lived it only breathed a little bit with the tides. When I first came to New York and looked out the window and saw the river flowing the wrong way, I checked a map, then a compass, and then I sat by the window feeling scared.

———

In sixth grade I learned that the bends in a river are not in the same place every year. The bends move down the river, with the water. I learned this the same year that the restaurant on Route 7 was burned for the insurance money. The same year that the Burmasters' barn was moved to a historic site, leaving only a square of bare dirt at the end of our road.

———

We lived on a hill, in one of the only houses by the river that was safe. The river flooded almost every year. We knew a family that lost their entire house to icy water more than once. I stood in their driveway looking at the piles of boards.

———

I was taking a ferry to the Aran Islands, which I had read about in *National Geographic*. The ferry ride was gray and empty. Something in the way I was comforted by the humming of the engine reminded me of him. The waves breaking over the iron. I realized that I wanted to be with him. I took an orange out of my pocket and held it up against the gray. I snapped a picture of the orange, and a picture of the huge iron links of the chain in the bow of the ferry.

———

When I come home to visit, familiar shops have fallen into themselves, and the windows are no longer transparent. The river, though, has the same smell. The smell of crayfish caught and forgotten in plastic cups to boil in the sun.

———

This spring the river rose above its banks and froze, so that now ice hangs like heavy umbrellas in the tallest trees. The field where we walked last spring through grass thick as honey is matted with fallen trees and broken ice.

———

I get lost in Rochester and end up at Great Falls where the Genesee pours past some burned buildings. I wonder if these buildings were whole when my parents lived here. I wonder if my mother ever walked down here. There is one building with no windows that seems to be losing itself to the river, one brick at a time.

———

I dreamed that water was bad for me. I was lifting a glass to my lips when I saw, suddenly and clearly, in the water itself, that it was hurting me.

How could I have gone so long without knowing? If only all those people had not said it was good for me!

I was permanently poisoned. I knew for sure that after so many years of drinking water, it must be in my blood.

When I woke up I saw a picture in the newspaper of a woman holding out hands covered in sores. "For 25 years the government along with UNICEF and other aid groups have weaned villagers from disease carrying pond water and helped them to sink pipes into underground aquifers. Overlooked was the naturally occurring arsenic that tainted those subterranean sources." She was poisoned, but the reason she was crying was that her husband didn't want her anymore.

—

*When a woman finally begins to write for herself,
Virginia Woolf wondered, what she will have to
say? And how will she say it?*

*"No doubt we shall find her knocking that into
shape for herself when she has the free use of her
limbs; and providing some new vehicle, not neces-
sarily in verse, for the poetry in her. For it is the
poetry that is still denied outlet. And I went on to
ponder how a woman nowadays would write a
poetic tragedy in five acts—would she use verse—
would she not use prose rather?"*

It is after I've told him that I can't come to live with him. I wake up in the middle of the night to find that he's decided my bed has to be moved. I'm shivering, pulling the blankets around me. He is standing, in his underwear, and tossing all my things, my books, my letters, my hair clips, from the edge of the bed to the other side of the room. "Your bed is in the wrong place," he tells me, "Why do you want it up against the heater and the window? It's too hot and too cold." He pulls the blankets off me and begins to shove the mattress towards the center of the room, mumbling, "I need a little moderation."

—

"I don't know...." He has been saying this over and over, ending every thought with it. Finally I ask him, "What don't you know?" He pauses. "Lots of things. Your favorite color, for example."

—

It is late, almost midnight. There is an old man sitting on a crate playing harmonica. As I pass, he finishes the song and pauses. He sighs and bows his head to think of the next song. By the time I have passed he is playing again.

—

"Whenever a tool is handled with ease and with a minimum of false motions, so that it will produce accurate and satisfactory results, it is handled in the right way. The constant aim of every carpenter, especially the apprentice, should be to eliminate false motions in everything he does."
-*Carpenter's Tools*, H. H. Seigele

—

We are standing by the bed where his grandmother is dying. Her mouth hangs open like an irregular pond and her head leans to the side. She is made of sticks and her wedding ring hangs around her finger like a hula hoop. One gesture is still intact. A tiny motion with one hand turns the ring so that the stone is on top. Her hand moves away and the stone slides back around to her palm.

———

Every Thanksgiving, my stepmother makes a sweet potato pie that no one eats. It stays in the refrigerator whole, with the rest of the leftovers, until someone throws it out. Even she won't take a piece, and she admits that she only makes it because there was always one when she was a girl. No one ate it then either.

———

We sat on a towel at the beach because it was vacation. He was worrying about renter's insurance. He doesn't like sand or hot sun, and I only like to swim but the water was too cold. "What is that sound?" I kept asking him. It was coming from the water. The sky thickened at the horizon and we saw some flashes of lightning. We realized that the sound was thunder being swallowed by the water.

———

I am helping Kristen pack. The floor is covered with all her beloved things: dried orange peels, clothespins, empty cigar boxes, turquoise scarves, rusted razor blades, used tea bags. I throw every rock I find out the window. "There are some things I have to bring," she says, fingering a thin yellow night-gown with two red stains, "I don't wear this, but I imagine myself in it, standing in a doorway in a foreign country... with the wind blowing." She laughs and puts it in her bag.

———

He's on stage. Through the cigar smoke and Christmas lights of the bar I watch one muscle in his arm. On the TV in the corner, which plays mutely under the music, a fish jumps. He stares at the fingers of the bass player. Bubbles rise on the blue screen, then the TV flickers and a motorcycle crashes. He smiles and hits the cymbal.

———

Sometimes he gives a little flourish with his fingers that makes me wonder if all his movements are a quiet performance.

———

My father told us stories about the magic fish that would grant us anything we wished for. The secret of the magic fish was that by the end of the story, every single time, we would realize we had wished for the wrong thing. If we asked the fish for an endless bag of candy, we would get candy that was so disgusting we would beg the fish to take it back.

———

My father wrote to me once, "I don't know what it is that makes me such a poor husband."

———

I pause before I dive into the water. I am not scared of drowning, I am scared of hidden things, silent machinery under the water. A giant metal fan beneath the surface of the reservoir.

———

He rocks back and forth as he plays, the bass player is sweating, some music falls off its stand. Their sounds are tripping over each other, angry and fast. When the bass stops, he opens his eyes. The bass player has torn a finger open. Years of callus ripped away. Bending his head against his drumsticks, he begins to cry.

———

We had been arguing for hours and it was dark in the room. We sat silently on the couch, I was tapping my foot against the table. He glanced at the green digital glow of the clock. "2:05 is beautiful," he said. I looked, and it was.

———

The milkweed on the hill has opened, all the pods yellow bird mouths, gaping, pouring out silky white tufts that fill the air. It is like a mistake. The mouths had frozen open and what should have been a sharp call turned into down and drifted off on the wind.

———

When he left I didn't say anything. I sat frozen and thought that every sound was him coming back. The wind blew my door open a little and it creaked, papers on my wall fluttered. I thought someone might be walking up the stairs. Two hours after he left, I looked out the window to see if he was standing there.

———

Allana says something quietly and Ben touches his hearing aid. Spinach is steaming on the stove. She leans a little closer to him.

———

I pass two old men in the park wearing fur hats, just as one is saying, "Your wife isn't coming back." The other is lighting a pipe. "What's to say she isn't coming back?"

———

He left the morning I had dreamt that the gas stove exploded. This was the first thing I told him when I woke up, before I realized how angry he was. In the dream I turned on one burner and heard the gas rushing out but it wouldn't light. I tried to turn it off but the dial was stuck. I turned on all the burners and none of them would light but none of them would turn back off. I could smell the gas. Then I heard the clicking of the stove getting ready to light.

———

He left a scrap of paper on my desk with a picture of a coin that said, "heads you win, tails you win."

———

I remember dancing with him. Water was boiling. His hair was newly cut. He was holding my hand and the kitchen light was bright. Someone was running the tap over a sink full of dirty dishes, and the door opened and shut with a heavy rush like feathers. Water was boiling. My cheek was soft against his warm chest and I liked the feeling of his stomach when it brushed mine. People were talking, I laughed and answered, and our feet kept moving, slowly.

———

I remember a wet runway, scattered with blue lights, the outlines of the planes hard to separate. They were lining up for takeoff. Giant, blinking animals inching forward, churning impatiently.

In my sleep I had a sense of us as huge and fragile, navigating the same bed. That is how we slept together that last night, hardly touching.

—

Women now face the task not only of finding a form that can express what they have lived, but of finding a way to tell new stories about what they can live. Carolyn Heilbrun suggests that the story of a revolutionary marriage has yet to be written. She writes that, "New definitions and a new reality about marriage must be not only lived but narrated." And must they be lived before they are narrated?

My father and I are driving home in the rain, I am watching his finger flick the windshield wipers on and off. "I remember the first time I rode in a car with intermittent wipers," he tells me, and I laugh. "I got a call to a house where a man had died in his sleep. My car broke down on the way and I had to hitch-hike. The paramedics refused to stop resuscitating the poor guy until I got there. They just kept working the dead body while the man's wife and kid watched. I finally made it and signed the death certificate. His son gave me a ride home. Really nice fellow. His car had intermittent wipers."

—

Letter: "I came home and found a dead pigeon on the doorstep with its head curled sweetly under its wing. I went inside to get a box for it because I thought I would give it to Kristen. When I came out again it was gone and I wondered if it had been dead after all.

"I once saw a show of photos that documented reconstructive plastic surgery. There is one I remember of a middle-aged woman with a face that was crooked but very handsome in a way. It seemed that she had been born with a deformed jaw, but her face had become accustomed to it.

"The next photo showed the same woman six months after plastic surgery. Her cheek was caved in, her nose was bent, her eyes were sunken and bruised and dark....None of that cutting could be undone.

"Should I write again?"

—

My father's musical instruments have been sitting unused in their cases for years. The banjo case stands in a dark corner, gray with dust, and my littlest sister doesn't even know what is in it. The trumpet and its case have disappeared entirely. The piano sits open, with the same sheet of music in its tray, "Basic Exercises."

—

Small things. One of the boards of my windowsill is not painted on the end. A bolt is missing from the railing, and my eyes keep going back to the place where it belongs. My mother wrote about the hole where the doorknob had been. "Ordinary pain."

—

There is a row of clocks, each with a different time for a different city. Chicago, New York, Tokyo….Every second hand jumps at a slightly different moment. The whole line of them quivers.

—

I am examining the texture of my doctor's ceiling when she asks me, "Do you ever experience the sensation of arrhythmia?" I smile.

—

When I tell him that I miss him he says, "It must be phantom pain."

—

One small leaf fell off my fig tree, tiny and fuzzy. I found a dead kitten in the road, its body still warm and loose. I buried it, leaving its head uncovered just in case it began to breathe again. I swam in the reservoir as it was getting dark. A couple stood on the edge before they took off their clothes. They held each other in the water, laughing, and the girl wrapped her legs around his waist. He carried her to shore like that.

—

He came on a Thursday evening. I was falling asleep early. The room was hot and he kept whispering, "You're real!"

—

There is hot water running into the sink. I am turning to talk to someone and my wrist, right below my palm, brushes the faucet, which is warm. My body remembers him and I can't say anything.

———

He sent me half of a letter, ripped down the middle. A week later, he sent me the other half. "A puzzle for you," he said over the phone, laughing. He sent me a page of a book with the word 'disillusion' circled.

———

I had the taste of envelopes in my mouth and I slept in my clothes for no reason. All day leaves blowing across the road looked like animals. Driving in the rain I sang, "As if I didn't know by now, as if I hadn't learned...."

———

Harry, whose wife had died long before he moved in with us, cut off his finger with the table saw. He clamped his handkerchief over the cut, but it didn't seem to hurt him much and he never spoke of it after the stump healed.

———

I see in the paper that a man who lost his hand fifteen years ago has been given a new one, transplanted from a cadaver. "Doctors said yesterday that the hand had turned pink and had shown signs of life."

———

Letter: "Emrah's tooth turned black in his mouth and he cried from the pain of it. I spent a whole night without sleep, trying to push you out of my mind. Emrah had his tooth extracted and was smiling tonight. I passed that point on Bay Road today, where the hills are yellow and very wide and I always think, 'I would like to drive all day,' and I kept driving with the heater on and the music and Rachel humming beside me. There was fog and a bit of rain, no line between the river and the sky. Five old sunflowers bent in a field. We stopped at the petting zoo to look in at the sad peacocks and I held my hand under a calf's nose so that Rachel could see his tongue when he licked me. Later, the light filtered through the mist like your long fingers."

———

I confess that once, after I watched a cat crawl up and fall asleep on his chest, I thought I might like to have a child with him.

———

In my dream I saw only white and the sentence, "leaving a tattoo like honey, honey..." repeated, looping over itself again and again.

———

He likes the word 'parallax,' which I look up in the dictionary: "The difference in apparent direction of an object as seen from two different points not on a straight line with the object."

———

I linger over one article in the newspaper: A story about distance. A doctor who had volunteered to give medical advice to sailors got a message, by computer, from a man sailing alone. He told the doctor that his arm was white and swollen, like a pillow. As soon as he got the message, in the late evening, the doctor wrote him instructions on how he had to operate. The man's computer was solar powered, so there was no more news until daylight. In the morning, the next message said, "I am sitting here in my own blood, my life is slipping...."

———

Every fall Harry would make honey. He knew by the color how it would taste and what kind of flower the bees had been gathering from. He took a hot knife in his shaking hand and drew it over the face of the comb. He gave us warm pieces of wax to chew the honey out of, and what I remember best is the ache in the back of my throat.

———

Stories are only true if we believe them. Or if we live them. It is unclear where our parents' stories end and where our stories begin.

My sister doesn't remember our father taking her into the bedroom after I demanded that he spank her and then whispering to her to yell every time he hit the bed with his belt. I was the one who heard her scream disintegrate into giggles, but what she remembers is a story Dad told about our grandfather taking him into the bedroom after he had ruined Grandma's new wallpaper. Grandpa looked Dad straight in the eye, slowly undid his belt, and said softly, "You better make some noise every time I hit this bed."

Five years ago, I took a picture of a little girl lying on her father, who was stretched out on a park bench, his cheek pressed against her cheek. For an instant the wind lifted up her hair and made a halo around them. The picture was taken at exactly the right moment, but there was no more film on the roll.

———

A Swiss psychiatrist and a British pilot finally made it around the world in a balloon. They miscalculated slightly and their journey ended in the desert, where they waited for hours. "It is wrong to think there is nothing in the desert," one said, "It is remarkable how well you can fill emptiness." The other said, "I'm very glad this is over."

———

The video camera was zippered into the bag, still on, and it recorded only blackness and a few points of light shining through the canvas. The audio recorded the sounds of the street, some pieces of conversation, and the static from a policeman's walkie-talkie.

———

We weren't talking to each other when he drove over the electric wire, and we said nothing as blue sparks the size of hands snapped across the hood. He kept driving and I twisted around in my seat to look back at the wire curling over the street.

———

"It's important that you wear a train with this, even if you don't want it for the reception," the woman in the bridal shop is telling a customer. "You have to get that mystical body entrance, that transcendental moment that combines the sacramental, the emotional, and the physical. After that, you can take it off."

———

So many fairy tales have been changed. They have been adapted for movies. The stories have been rewritten so that the woman who steps out of the ocean, perfect and naked, does not slip back into the skin of a seal. Cartoon fairy tales end in a shower of flower petals falling over a wedding as the credits begin. They should end with the woman disappearing into the sea.
